The Cane Part 2: The Summoning

Elias Von Slaught awoke in a cold sweat, his heart racing. His parents' faces were still fresh in his mind—twisted in agony, their voices calling out to him from a place beyond the veil of dreams. The image of his father's cane loomed over them, glowing faintly, as if it were the only thing keeping them tethered to the world. But in the dream, no matter how hard Elias reached for it, the cane stayed just out of his grasp.

He sat up in bed, trying to shake off the remnants of the nightmare. But the sense of dread clung to him. It wasn't the first time he had dreamt of the cane—it had been weeks now, ever since his parents stopped answering his calls. At first, he brushed it off, thinking they were traveling or busy with work, but now, he wasn't so sure. There was something different about this dream, something more real, more urgent. The cane wasn't just an artifact from his father's past—it was a link to whatever had happened to them.

Elias glanced at his phone on the bedside table. No missed calls. No messages. Just the same eerie silence that had followed him for days. He couldn't ignore it any longer. His parents were in trouble, and the cane was the key to finding them.

He got out of bed and paced the room, his mind racing. He knew where the cane was—his father always kept it in the study, locked away in a glass cabinet. The last time he'd seen it, it had looked so ordinary, like any other walking stick. But now, it was different. The dream had shown him something, something he hadn't understood before.

Determined, Elias grabbed his jacket and keys. He had to see the cane for himself, had to know if the dream was real. His parents had always kept secrets, but this was one he couldn't let remain hidden any longer.

As he left his apartment and headed toward his childhood home, the air felt heavier, the night quieter than usual. It was as if the world was holding its breath, waiting for something to happen. And deep down, Elias knew that whatever came next, his life would never be the same again.

He arrived at the house, the familiar creak of the front door almost comforting. The study was just as he remembered, everything in its place. But the cabinet with the cane drew his attention immediately. The glass seemed to shimmer, and as he approached, he felt a strange vibration in the air. Slowly, he reached for the key to unlock it.

The moment his fingers touched the cane, a shock of energy pulsed through him, and the room seemed to tilt. His vision blurred, and for a brief second, he saw his parents again, trapped in darkness, calling his name.

Elias stumbled back, his heart pounding. The dream hadn't been just a dream. His parents were out there—somewhere. And the cane was the only way to find them.

He stood there for a moment, staring at the cane, his mind spinning. He didn't know what to do next. The cane held some kind of power, that much was clear, but how could he use it? His father had never spoken about its true nature, and his mother had been even more distant when it came to discussing family matters. How was he supposed to figure this out on his own?

His thoughts raced. He couldn't afford to waste time. His parents were in danger, and he needed answers fast. Then, a flicker of memory surfaced—his mother had once mentioned her uncle, a reclusive man living in Romania. She hadn't spoken about him much, but Elias remembered hearing something about his deep knowledge of the family's strange history. If anyone knew something about the cane's power, it might be him.

Elias rushed to his mother's study, rummaging through her things, hoping to find some sort of contact information. He pulled open drawers, flipping through old papers, calendars, and notebooks, his hands trembling. After several frantic minutes, he found her personal calendar. It was filled with appointments, scribbled notes, and phone numbers, many of which seemed outdated.

His fingers hovered over a name: Uncle Drago – Romania. Next to it, a phone number.

Elias felt a flicker of hope. He didn't know much about Uncle Drago, but he was his only lead. He grabbed his phone, his hands shaking as he dialed the number. Would this man have the answers he so desperately needed?

The line rang, and Elias held his breath, waiting for someone to pick up.

Elias stood in the quiet, his mind racing. Going to Romania on a whim seemed reckless, but what other option did he have? Unsure, he decided he needed a second opinion. His old friend Christian had always been good at helping him think through tough situations. If anyone could help him figure out what to do, it would be Christian.

He quickly dialed Christian's number, expecting to hear his familiar voice on the other end. Instead, the line went dead after a few rings. Frowning, Elias tried again, but this time, the phone gave a long beep before an automated message came on: "This number is no longer in service."

"That's strange," Elias muttered. He hadn't spoken to Christian in a while, but it wasn't like him to disappear without a word. Maybe he'd changed his number? Then it hit him—Christian had a sister, Joanne. If anyone knew where Christian was, it would be her.

"What was her number again?" Elias mumbled to himself. He dug through his old contacts, finally finding Joanne's name buried in the list. He hesitated for a moment, unsure if she would remember him, but then pressed the call button. He needed to know what had happened to Christian, and Joanne was his only link to finding out.

Elias waited as the phone rang. After a few moments, a soft voice answered.

"Hello?" a woman said.

"Jo?" Elias asked, feeling a small surge of hope.

"Yes," she responded.

"Hey, it's Elias... Christian's old friend. Do you remember me?"

There was a pause, but then Jo's tone shifted, a hint of recognition in her voice. "Of course I do, Elias! How are you?"

Before Elias could respond, he heard the faint sound of a child giggling in the background, followed by a man's voice, playfully talking to the child. The joyful sounds felt out of place against the weight of the conversation he was about to have, but he tried to focus.

"I've been... well, it's been a strange time," Elias continued, his voice uncertain. "I've been trying to get in touch with Christian, but his number's disconnected. I was hoping you could help me reach him."

There was a long silence on the other end. Then, Jo's voice softened. "Elias, I—I thought you knew. Christian passed away six months ago."

The words hit him like a punch to the gut. "What? No... I didn't know. How did it happen?"

The sound of the toddler's laughter carried faintly through the phone again, followed by the man's playful murmurs. Jo took a shaky breath before speaking again. "It was an accident. We went camping for my birthday... something happened out there, something I still can't explain. Christian didn't make it back."

Elias could hear the strain in her voice, the weight of what she was carrying. "What do you mean, something happened?"

Jo was quiet for a moment, and the background noise of the child and man playing seemed to fade. When she spoke again, her voice was shaky. "There was a clearing—it didn't feel right. We found a stone with strange markings on it. After that, everything went dark. Christian tried to protect me, but something woke up that night. Something took him."

Elias stood frozen, his mind spinning. He thought of the shimmering cane, the dark sense of dread that had been haunting him. Could the same forces that had taken his parents be the same thing that took Christian?

"I'm so sorry, Jo," Elias said softly. "But I think whatever happened to Christian might be connected to my parents' disappearance. They've vanished, and the cane—my father's cane

—it's glowing. I don't know what it means, but I'm going to Romania to talk to my uncle. He might know something."

Jo was silent for a moment, the background sounds of the child and man playing again creeping into the conversation. "Christian mentioned the cane once before the trip," Jo said, her voice quieter now. "He said it reminded him of the markings on the stone we found. Do you think... do you think the same thing that took him is coming for your parents?"

Elias hesitated. "I don't know, but I need answers. I think I'm going to need your help too, Jo. Whatever happened to Christian, whatever this thing is, we need to find out the truth."

The playful laughter of the child faded into a distant hum, and Jo sighed, her voice heavy with grief. "I don't know if I can face it again, Elias. But if it means getting answers about what happened to Christian... I'll try. Just be careful, okay? I've already lost my brother. I can't lose anyone else."

Elias listened as the sounds of the toddler's laughter faded into the background. "You have a child?" he asked, surprised by this unexpected glimpse into Jo's new life.

"Yes, a little girl. She's 3 months old now," Jo said, her voice warm with pride.

"That's wonderful, Jo," Elias responded, a smile briefly touching his lips. "And you're married too?"

"Yes, I am," Jo replied. "Life has been full of changes, despite everything that happened."

"That's great news," Elias said sincerely, though his thoughts began to churn. As much as he was happy for her, the weight of what he had to face quickly returned. With a child and a husband, how could he involve her in this dangerous journey? Whatever force had taken Christian—and now his parents—was too dark, too dangerous to drag her into. He hesitated, choosing his words carefully. "Jo, I'm really glad to hear you're doing well. But maybe... maybe it's best if you stay out of this. You've got a family now, and I don't want to put you at risk."

Jo was quiet for a moment, considering his words. "I get it, Elias," she said softly. "I really do. But you shouldn't do this alone."

Before Elias could respond, Jo continued. "There's someone who might be able to help, though. My friend Teresa... she's been through some strange stuff herself, things that sound a lot like what's happening to you. She's strong, and she's got experience with... well, things that are hard to explain. If anyone could help you, it's her."

"Teresa?" Elias asked, uncertain. "What kind of experience?"

"Let's just say she knows how to handle the supernatural," Jo replied. "She might be exactly who you need to talk to."

Elias thought for a moment, considering the possibility. "Alright," he finally said. "I'll reach out to her. Thanks, Jo."

Jo let out a soft sigh of relief. "Just be careful, Elias. Whatever you're dealing with, it's dangerous. I don't want to lose anyone else."

"You won't," Elias promised, though he wasn't sure if he believed it himself. The path ahead seemed darker and more uncertain than ever, but at least now he had a direction—and someone who might just be able to help.

Jo's voice softened again. "Elias, if you're going to be in the middle of all this, maybe we should meet up. If you're coming to Chicago anytime soon, we could talk more in person. I think it might help, and I could introduce you to Teresa."

Elias thought for a moment. "Actually, I could be there tomorrow. I've been meaning to follow up on some things, and I think seeing you would be a good start."

Jo sounded relieved. "Great. Let's meet the day after you arrive, then. How about we meet at a café? There's one downtown I like, Café Vienna. We can meet there and talk through everything."

"That sounds good," Elias agreed. "I'll be in Chicago tomorrow, and we'll meet the next day. Around noon?"

"Perfect," Jo replied. "Be safe, Elias."

"You too, Jo. I'll see you soon," he said before they hung up.

As he placed the phone down, Elias felt a strange mix of relief and anxiety. His journey was about to begin, and the stakes were higher than ever.

At this point, Elias had completely forgotten about his uncle Drago. His thoughts were entirely focused on Jo and the possibility of finally getting some answers about the strange and dangerous world he had been thrust into. Seeing Jo after everything that had happened filled him with a strange sense of hope—maybe, just maybe, he was close to understanding what had taken Christian and his parents.

Before leaving for Chicago, Elias made sure everything at his parents' home was secure. He checked all the doors and windows, ensuring they were locked, and set the alarm. With one last glance at the now-empty house, he turned and headed back to his apartment.

Once home, he began packing for his trip. His mind buzzed with anticipation, the thought of meeting Jo again after so long mixing with the need for answers. This trip to Chicago wasn't just a reunion—it could be the key to unlocking the mysteries surrounding the cane, Christian's death, and his parents' disappearance.

With his bag packed and his plan set, Elias felt the gravity of the situation settle over him again. This was only the beginning, but it felt like the pieces were finally falling into place.

Elias had always known his family carried secrets, but as he prepared to leave for Chicago, the weight of those mysteries pressed heavier on his mind. He couldn't shake the feeling that his parents' disappearance, Christian's death, and the strange powers of the cane were all connected by something much darker than he had first imagined.

The flight to Chicago was a blur of anxiety. He kept replaying Jo's voice in his head—how she had described the markings on the stone that echoed the designs on the cane. And Teresa. Who was she? How could someone who seemed so disconnected from his world be the key to unraveling these mysteries?

By the time Elias landed in Chicago, the city's gray autumn sky matched the heaviness he felt inside. He couldn't delay anymore. He needed answers, and soon.

The next day, he arrived early at Café Vienna, its warm, wood-paneled walls a stark contrast to the chilly breeze outside. The air was filled with the comforting scent of freshly brewed coffee and pastries. He sat near the back, where he had a clear view of the entrance, nervously drumming his fingers on the table. He wasn't sure what to expect from Jo after all these years, especially after learning about Christian's death and everything she had been through.

Finally, the door swung open, and Jo walked in. She looked different, yet familiar—older, more grounded, but with the same determined spark in her eyes that Elias remembered from their youth. She spotted him immediately and made her way to his table.

"Hey," she said with a soft smile, sitting down. Her voice had a warmth to it, though there was an underlying tension, as if she were carrying too much weight.

"Hey, Jo," Elias replied, his voice a little unsteady. "It's good to see you again. I'm so sorry... about Christian."

Jo's expression tightened slightly, and she nodded. "Thank you. It's been hard. Harder than I thought. But you're here now, and that means something." She looked at him carefully. "I heard from Teresa after we talked. She's willing to meet you."

"That's good," Elias said, feeling a slight sense of relief. "I don't even know what I'm dealing with, Jo. Everything is just... it feels like it's spiraling out of control. The cane, my parents' disappearance, Christian—it's all connected, I know it. I just don't understand how."

Jo leaned back slightly, her face clouded with thought. "Teresa... she's seen things, Elias. Things most people would never believe. When I told her about what happened to Christian, she wasn't even surprised. It's like she already knew something like that could happen. I don't know how she'll help, but I trust her."

Elias nodded, feeling the weight of Jo's words. "Where is she?"

"She'll meet us tonight," Jo replied. "But I need to ask you—are you sure you want to go through with this? Whatever this is, it's dangerous. More dangerous than I realized when we went on that camping trip. I don't want to lose anyone else."

Elias swallowed hard, the memories of his parents' faces in the dream flashing through his mind. "I don't have a choice, Jo. If I don't do this, I'll lose them for good. I can feel it."

Jo studied him for a long moment, then nodded. "Alright. Let's do this, then."

Later that evening, Elias and Jo arrived at a small, unmarked bookstore tucked away on a quiet street. It didn't look like much, but Jo assured him this was where they were meeting

Teresa. The old wooden sign above the door creaked in the wind, and the dim light from inside gave the place an eerie, almost timeless quality.

Jo led the way inside, where the scent of old paper and leather greeted them. Shelves filled with dusty tomes stretched to the ceiling, and in the corner sat a small reading area with a single figure waiting for them. Teresa.

She was younger than Elias expected, maybe in her late twenties, with sharp eyes that seemed to carry the weight of many lives' worth of experience. As they approached, she stood up, her movements graceful and deliberate.

"You must be Elias," Teresa said, her voice soft but firm. She extended a hand, and as Elias took it, he felt a strange, almost electric current pass between them.

"Yes," Elias replied, feeling a little off-balance. "Thank you for meeting with us."

Teresa nodded, glancing at Jo before turning her attention fully to Elias. "Jo told me about what's been happening, about Christian and the cane. I believe you're dealing with something much older than any of us realize. Something dark."

Elias shifted uneasily. "What do you know about it?"

"Not enough," Teresa admitted, her eyes narrowing slightly. "But I've encountered similar forces before. Old magic. Things people have forgotten, or at least, wish they could forget. But there's always a price when those forces are disturbed. And it sounds like your family's history is tied to something much older—something that wants to stay hidden."

Elias felt a chill run down his spine. "So what do we do?"

"We start by learning what we can about the cane," Teresa said, her voice taking on a determined edge. "There's power in it, but power like that is never simple. It's tied to something—perhaps a curse, or a pact. We need to figure out how it works, and why it's affecting your family."

Elias nodded, feeling a sense of purpose rise within him. Finally, he wasn't alone in this.

Teresa gestured to the back of the shop. "I have some things I want to show you. It might help us understand the forces we're up against."

As they followed Teresa into the deeper, darker corners of the bookstore, Elias couldn't shake the feeling that this was only the beginning. Whatever they uncovered here would likely lead to even greater dangers. But he had no choice. His parents' lives—and perhaps much more—depended on it.

As Teresa led them further into the bookstore, Elias noticed the shelves growing more sparse, the air cooler, as if they were entering a different world. Finally, they reached a small, candlelit alcove with an old, wooden table in the center. Scattered across it were books and strange objects—items Elias couldn't identify but felt drawn to nonetheless.

Teresa motioned for them to sit, and she pulled an old, worn-out leather-bound book toward her. "This is something I've been studying for years," she said, her eyes serious. "It's one of the few sources I've found that talks about the kind of magic your family's cane might be tied to."

Jo shifted in her seat, glancing at Elias. "What exactly are we dealing with?"

Teresa took a deep breath before responding. "We're dealing with something ancient. In my case, I was cursed—my family in the Philippines had a dark history that stretched back generations. The curse of the *Aswang*, a creature that takes many forms and feeds on the living, is something I've carried with me all my life. My mother's death and my return to Capiz stirred something. But moving to the United States didn't free me from it. It followed me, and I've had to learn how to control it, to survive."

Elias stared at her, stunned. He hadn't expected Teresa to share something so deeply personal, but now, he understood why Jo had trusted her. She wasn't just knowledgeable about the supernatural; she had lived it.

Teresa continued, her voice steady. "The *Aswang* curse is different from what you're facing, but I've learned that these forces—curses, dark magic—are all part of the same world. Your father's cane... it's not just a relic. It's likely tied to a pact or a curse, something your family may have been involved with for generations, even if they didn't realize it."

Elias leaned forward, trying to take it all in. "So, the cane... it's connected to whatever took my parents. And Christian too."

Teresa nodded. "Yes, but there's more. The dream you had—about the cane glowing and your parents calling out to you—that's not just a dream. It's a message. Your parents are trapped in a place between life and death. The cane is the key to reaching them, but there's a cost. Magic like this always demands something in return."

Jo's face paled slightly. "What kind of cost?"

Teresa met Jo's gaze, her expression somber. "The cost could be anything. It could demand a sacrifice, or it could try to claim Elias himself. These forces... they don't let go easily."

Elias felt a knot tighten in his stomach. "So how do we stop it?"

"We need to understand the origins of the cane," Teresa said, flipping through the old book. "If we can figure out where it came from, who made it, and why, we might be able to undo the magic that binds it. But it won't be easy."

Elias's mind flashed back to something his mother had said in passing, years ago—about their family's roots in Eastern Europe. His uncle Drago had always seemed like an enigma, someone his parents rarely talked about. But he had to know something. Maybe he had been part of this all along.

"Uncle Drago," Elias said suddenly. "He's my mother's uncle. He lives in Romania. My mom always said he knew more about the family's history than anyone else. I tried to reach him, but..." He hesitated. "I didn't follow up. I got sidetracked."

Teresa raised an eyebrow, clearly intrigued. "Drago. I've heard the name before." She leaned back slightly, her fingers brushing over the strange objects on the table. "Your uncle could be the key to understanding the cane. But you need to be careful. If he's tied to the same magic, he may not be trustworthy."

Elias swallowed hard, the weight of the situation pressing down on him. He had always thought of Uncle Drago as this distant, eccentric relative—someone who lived in the old world, disconnected from modern life. But now, he realized Drago might be far more dangerous than he had imagined.

"What do you know about him?" Elias asked, his voice tense.

Teresa didn't answer immediately. Instead, she stood up and moved to a nearby shelf, pulling down a large, heavy book. She opened it to a page marked by an old ribbon and turned it toward Elias and Jo. There, in faded ink, was an illustration of a man holding a staff that looked eerily similar to his father's cane. The man's face was shadowed, but something about the way he was drawn sent a chill through Elias.

"Drago's name comes up in various places," Teresa said quietly. "He's been involved in... things. Dark things. Some say he's a practitioner of old magic, others believe he's a guardian of sorts, protecting his family from curses. But the truth is likely more complicated."

Jo leaned in, studying the page. "So, he could be the one who cursed Elias's family? Or he could be the one protecting them?"

Teresa shrugged slightly. "Possibly both. Magic isn't always as clear-cut as good and evil. It's layered in intent and consequence. Drago may have been trying to protect the family by binding them to the cane, but over time, that magic could have twisted into something more dangerous."

Elias felt a mix of anger and confusion. His parents were missing, Christian was dead, and now it seemed his family had been tied to something sinister for generations. He didn't know whether to trust Uncle Drago—or fear him.

"So, what do we do now?" he asked.

Teresa closed the book, her eyes steady and focused. "First, we need to find out more about Drago and the history of the cane. Then, we prepare. There's a ritual I know that could help you connect more deeply with the cane's magic, but it's risky. If you're willing to take that risk, it could give us the answers we need to save your parents."

Elias didn't hesitate. "I'll do whatever it takes."

Elias sat quietly as Teresa laid out the preparations for the ritual. The air in the bookstore felt heavier now, charged with anticipation. Teresa lit several candles, their flickering light casting long shadows on the walls. In the center of the table sat the cane, its wooden surface worn and polished from years of use. Teresa had asked Elias to bring it from his parents' home, and now it rested between them, as though waiting for the secrets it held to be unlocked.

"Are you ready?" Teresa asked, her voice steady but cautious.

Elias nodded, though his heart raced. He wasn't sure what to expect, but he knew this was his only chance—at least for now—to reach his parents.

Teresa placed a small bowl in front of him, filled with a mixture of herbs and oils that smelled pungent and earthy. "This will help connect you to the cane's magic," she explained. "It may feel disorienting at first, but you need to stay focused on your parents. Visualize them—where they are, how they're feeling. The cane will guide you."

Elias swallowed hard and closed his eyes as Teresa began to chant in a language he didn't recognize. The words felt ancient, almost like a hum vibrating through the air. Slowly, the scent of the herbs and oils filled his senses, and the world around him seemed to fade.

For a moment, he felt a pull—like a tether—drawing him toward the cane. His mind blurred, and in the darkness, he saw faint images of his parents, their faces distorted by shadows. They were reaching out to him, calling his name, but no matter how hard he tried, the distance between them remained. The glow of the cane flickered weakly, as though struggling to maintain the connection.

Then, without warning, everything went dark.

Elias gasped, opening his eyes. He was back in the bookstore, the candles still flickering softly around him. His heart pounded in his chest as he glanced at Teresa, who was watching him with a calm but concerned expression.

"It didn't work," Elias muttered, frustration tightening his voice. "I saw them, but they were... too far. I couldn't reach them."

Teresa nodded slowly, her face thoughtful. "The cane's power is strong, but something is blocking you. I think whatever magic binds your parents is tied more deeply to your family's past than we initially thought."

Elias's thoughts drifted to his uncle Drago. There was no avoiding it now—his mother's cryptic comments about Drago's knowledge of their family's history had to be connected to the cane. And if the ritual didn't work here, maybe the answers were in Romania, where his family's roots—and Drago—awaited.

"I think... I think I need to go to Romania," Elias said, the words falling from his lips before he had fully considered them. "Drago—my uncle. He's invited me before, but I've always stayed away. Now I don't think I have a choice. He's involved in this somehow."

Teresa's eyes narrowed as she considered his words. "If Drago knows about the cane, he might be the key to unlocking its full power. But he's dangerous, Elias. If you go, you'll be walking into a situation where you may not know who to trust."

"I have to try," Elias said, his voice firm. "He's my only lead. And if he's involved in whatever curse or pact is tied to my family, then he's the one who can help me figure out how to break it."

Teresa leaned back in her chair, folding her arms across her chest. "If you're going to Romania, I'm coming with you."

Elias blinked in surprise. "You'd do that?"

"Yes," Teresa replied without hesitation. "I've faced dark forces before. I've survived them. I know how to protect myself—and you. If your uncle is as dangerous as I think he is, you're going to need help. Besides, I owe it to Jo. She asked me to help you, and I take that seriously."

Elias was silent for a moment, taking in her offer. He hadn't expected Teresa to be so willing to dive into something this dangerous, but the relief he felt knowing he wouldn't have to face this alone was undeniable.

"Thank you," Elias said, his voice filled with gratitude. "I don't know what we'll find, but having you there—it makes me feel like I've got a chance."

Teresa smiled faintly, though her eyes remained serious. "We'll figure this out. But we need to be careful. Drago might be the key to unlocking the curse, but if he's kept his distance all these years, there's a reason for that. You need to be prepared for anything."

Elias nodded. "I understand. I'll make the arrangements. We'll leave as soon as possible."

As they stood to leave the bookstore, Elias felt a mixture of fear and determination rising within him. The ritual may have failed, but the path forward was clear now. Romania, his family's past, and Drago—they were all tied to the fate of his parents, and whatever dark forces had bound them. And with Teresa by his side, he knew he wouldn't face it alone.

Elias embraced Jo warmly outside the café, the weight of their shared grief hanging in the air between them. He held her a moment longer than expected, feeling the comfort of her friendship despite the dark circumstances that had brought them back together.

"Take care of yourself, Jo," Elias whispered, pulling away with a sad smile. "I hope you find peace."

Jo nodded, her eyes moist but resolute. "You too, Elias. Be careful in Romania. And... if you need anything, just let me know."

With that, they parted ways, and Elias turned to Teresa, who had been standing a few paces away, giving them space. Together, they headed to his hotel, the cool night air brushing against them as they walked in silence.

As they entered the quiet of his hotel room, Elias couldn't help but glance at Teresa, his mind briefly drifting away from the supernatural burden weighing them down. There was something magnetic about her presence, and he couldn't deny it. Teresa was a strikingly beautiful woman, her features sharp yet delicate, with a certain intensity in her almond-shaped eyes that made her seem wiser than her years. Her smooth, caramel-toned skin gleamed softly in the dim light of the room, and her long, dark hair framed her face in gentle waves, falling gracefully past her shoulders.

She moved with a kind of effortless elegance, her every gesture precise, controlled. Dressed in simple, practical clothes, she still carried a sense of quiet confidence, as though her beauty was just a small part of her powerful presence. There was a strength in her that made it clear she had faced—and survived—things few could imagine.

Elias couldn't help but think, *If this were a different time, a different place, things might have been different between us.* But he quickly pushed the thought aside. They were here for a purpose, and the dangers they faced left no room for personal distractions.

Teresa caught him looking at her and raised an eyebrow, a slight smile tugging at the corner of her lips. "Something on your mind?"

Elias cleared his throat, feeling a bit awkward under her gaze. "Just... thinking about everything we have ahead of us," he said, not entirely untruthfully.

Teresa's smile widened for a moment before she nodded, her expression becoming serious again. "We'll get through it, Elias. One way or another."

Elias admired her determination, her beauty now secondary to the confidence and wisdom she exuded. He knew having her by his side was a blessing—she was someone who not only understood the supernatural world but could stand strong against it.

"Let's rest while we can," Teresa said, her voice soft but resolute. "Tomorrow's going to be a long day."

Elias nodded in agreement, his thoughts still lingering on the complexities of their situation—and the enigmatic woman standing beside him.

Elias and Teresa arrived at Chicago O'Hare Airport, the bustling atmosphere enveloping them as they checked in for their flight to Bucharest. The wait was longer than they expected, with two hours before their flight was set to take off. After collecting their boarding passes, they headed toward the TSA checkpoint, joining the long line of travelers snaking through the terminal.

The line moved slowly, giving Elias time to feel the weight of the journey ahead. He glanced at Teresa, who seemed calm and collected, her sharp eyes scanning their surroundings. She had an air of confidence, as though she had faced far worse than a long security line, and he admired her quiet strength.

Finally, they reached the TSA agents, who checked their IDs and waved them forward. They placed their belongings on the conveyor belt, shoes off, laptops and small personal items in separate trays, and walked through the scanners. A quick inspection later, they collected their things and moved on, making their way toward the terminal's restaurants.

The smell of food filled the air, and Elias's stomach rumbled. He realized he hadn't eaten since that morning, and the weight of anticipation had made him forget his hunger. Teresa seemed to notice his expression and gestured toward a cozy-looking Italian restaurant nearby.

"How about here?" she suggested, raising an eyebrow.

Elias nodded, following her inside, where they found a small table by the window overlooking the busy terminal. As they waited for their food, Teresa leaned back in her chair, studying him with a thoughtful expression.

"You're quiet," she said, breaking the silence.

Elias shrugged, his mind still reeling from everything they were about to face. "Just... everything is starting to feel real now. I don't know what to expect in Romania. I keep thinking about Drago and what I'll find."

Teresa nodded, her expression softening. "I understand. It's unsettling, facing something unknown." She paused, as if weighing her next words. "That's how I felt when I first faced the curse that haunted my family."

Elias looked at her, curiosity flickering in his eyes. "You've mentioned the curse before, but... what happened to you, Teresa?"

She took a deep breath, her gaze turning inward, as though she were looking back on memories she rarely shared. "I grew up in Capiz, a place known for stories about creatures from the other world. But it wasn't just stories for my family. We were cursed—cursed with the blood of an *Aswang*"

Elias's brow furrowed. "*Aswang*?"

Teresa nodded, her voice steady. "An *Aswang* is a creature that can take many forms—a vampire, a ghoul, a shapeshifter. In the Philippines, people grow up fearing these creatures, but for me, it wasn't just a fear. It was my reality. The curse ran through my mother's bloodline, passed down from generation to generation."

She paused as the server placed their dishes on the table, steaming plates of pasta and a shared basket of bread between them. After thanking the server, Teresa continued, her tone solemn.

"My mother knew about it but never spoke of it, trying to protect me, I suppose. But when she died, I had no choice but to move to my relatives in Chicago, thinking I could leave it all behind if I just... moved on. But curses like ours don't disappear. They follow you, whether you want them to or not."

Elias listened, mesmerized. "So... what happened?"

Teresa's fingers tightened around her glass. "I thought I could escape it by coming to the U.S., but the curse followed me. The first time I felt it... I was walking the banks and almost killed Jo and Jon. And after I realized what I was doing I managed to control myself and save them by pulling away. Once home I remember looking in the mirror and feeling this... darkness rising within me, something I couldn't control.

Elias shook his head, stunned. "You're... living with it even now?

"No, my father whom is a sorcerer helped me get rid of it but I can still feel the, who should I say this. "residue" of the creature inside me. Every day is a struggle, but it's also given me strength. Strength to face things most people would run from. That's why I agreed to come with you, Elias." Her voice softened. "I know what it's like to confront darkness head-on, to live with something you don't understand but know you have to fight."

They ate in silence for a few moments, the weight of her story settling between them. Elias could see the strength in her, the resilience that had kept her going despite everything she had faced. It made him feel grateful she was with him, that he wasn't facing this alone.

"Thank you for sharing that with me," he said quietly. "It's... a lot to carry. I had no idea."

Teresa gave a small smile, her eyes meeting his. "It's part of who I am. And in some strange way, I think it's what brought me here—to help you."

Elias reached across the table, placing his hand over hers for a brief moment. "Whatever waiting for us in Romania, I know I'm in good company."

She smiled softly. "We're in this together."

The announcement for their flight echoed through the terminal, calling them to board. They paid their bill and stood, grabbing their bags. As they headed toward the gate, Elias felt a sense of determination rising within him. The path was dark and uncertain, but he knew he could face it—with Teresa by his side.

Elias and Teresa boarded the plane, finding their seats in the quiet of the cabin as the lights dimmed for takeoff. The journey to Romania felt monumental, as if crossing an unseen threshold into a place where all the answers—and perhaps more dangers—waited.

As they settled in, Elias glanced at Teresa, who had closed her eyes, her face serene. He wondered how she managed to stay so calm. For him, the journey was filled with tension and unknowns, but Teresa seemed as grounded as ever. Perhaps it was her years of living with the curse, facing the darkness that followed her, that gave her such quiet confidence.

He couldn't help but feel a flicker of admiration—and, if he was honest with himself, a trace of something deeper. She was unlike anyone he'd ever met, her strength and beauty equally captivating.

The plane began to taxi down the runway, and Teresa opened her eyes, catching him watching her. She gave him a small, knowing smile.

"Penny for your thoughts?" she asked, her voice light.

Elias cleared his throat, suddenly aware of the intensity of his gaze. "Just... thinking about what we'll find when we land."

Teresa nodded, the seriousness returning to her eyes. "I've been wondering the same thing. But whatever it is, we're ready."

As the plane lifted off into the night, they both fell into silence, each lost in their own thoughts. For Elias, the memories of his parents' faces haunted him still, twisted in agony, calling out to him in desperation. And the cane—its faint glow in his dream, as if it were alive, watching him, holding secrets he was meant to uncover.

The hours passed in a blur, and Elias eventually drifted off, his mind too exhausted to keep him awake. Images flashed in his dreams—dark forests, shadows creeping at the edges of his vision, and a cold voice whispering his name. He felt a tugging sensation, as if something or someone were drawing him deeper into the darkness.

When he awoke, the sky outside was pale with the first hints of morning light, casting a soft glow over the cabin. He glanced at Teresa, who seemed to be sleeping peacefully beside him, her breathing steady and calm.

As they approached Bucharest, Elias felt a growing sense of anticipation mixed with dread. Romania held the key to everything, he was sure of it. And somewhere, in the heart of this foreign land, was Uncle Drago—waiting, watching, perhaps even aware of their arrival.

Upon landing, they collected their bags and made their way through customs, the formalities quick and efficient. Soon, they were outside the airport, breathing in the crisp, unfamiliar air of Romania.

Elias hailed a taxi, giving the driver the address of the small inn they had booked. As the car wound through the narrow streets of Bucharest, Elias couldn't shake the feeling that they were being watched, as though shadows themselves were alive, hiding secrets within their depths.

Finally, they reached the inn—a modest, historic building nestled among a row of stone-faced houses. The old-world charm of the place seemed to echo the mystery that surrounded their journey. Once they were checked in, they settled in their rooms, taking a moment to freshen up before meeting in the small lobby to discuss their plan.

"So, what's our next step?" Elias asked, his voice hushed.

Teresa pulled a piece of paper from her bag—a map with markings leading into a more remote part of the country. "I did some research before we left. There's a region a few hours north of here, close to the Carpathians, where Drago supposedly lives. If the cane is connected to him, then the answers we need are likely waiting for us there."

Elias felt a chill at the mention of the Carpathians, the mountain range steeped in folklore and legend. It was the perfect setting for the darkness that surrounded his family's curse.

"Do you think he'll help us?" Elias asked, uncertain.

Teresa looked at him, her eyes filled with both caution and determination. "I think he'll try. But his help may come with a cost. People who meddle in old magic don't usually come out unscathed."

Elias swallowed, the weight of her words settling over him. Whatever price Uncle Drago might demand, he was willing to pay it if it meant saving his parents.

As Elias pulled out his phone to call his uncle, a wave of unease settled over him. It was strange that he hadn't heard from Drago, especially considering the urgency of the situation. He dialed the number he'd saved from his mother's old notes and waited as it rang. After a few moments, the call went to voicemail.

"Hi, Uncle Drago, it's Elias," he began, trying to keep his voice steady. "I... I'm in Romania. I'm here with a friend, and we're coming to see you. Please call me back when you get this. I really need your help."

He ended the call and slipped the phone back into his pocket, feeling a small knot of frustration. The silence from his uncle was unsettling, like a missing piece in a puzzle that refused to fit. Elias pulled out the note his mother had left him, double-checking Drago's address. It was in a remote village in the Carpathians—a place Elias had never heard of.

But before he could start planning their route, Teresa gave him a gentle tap on the shoulder. "Don't worry about the hotel," she said, her tone practical yet reassuring. "I already booked one for us before we left Chicago. It's nearby, and I thought it would be best to settle in first before heading to your uncle's place."

Elias felt a surge of admiration. Teresa always seemed to be several steps ahead, her organized mind piecing everything together with precision and care. She was, without a doubt, the most prepared and capable person he'd ever met. He couldn't help but smile, grateful for her presence.

"You're incredible, you know that?" he said, shaking his head with a smile.

Teresa gave a soft laugh, a faint blush rising to her cheeks. "Just making sure we're ready for whatever comes next. I think we both know we need to be prepared."

With a nod, they gathered their bags and hailed another taxi to the hotel. As they settled in, Elias felt a strange sense of calm. Whatever lay ahead with Uncle Drago, he knew they were as prepared as they could be, and with Teresa by his side, he felt ready to face the unknown.

Elias raised his hand to hail a cab, his voice carrying a bit louder than he intended as he called out, "Taxi!" Two cabs zoomed past, each one ignoring him. Frustration was just beginning to settle in when, finally, a third cab pulled up and slowed to a stop.

As Elias bent down to get into the cab, his foot caught the edge of the curb, and he stumbled forward, nearly hitting the ground. He felt a firm hand on his shoulder, steadying him, but before he could react, he heard a soft, melodic laugh. He turned to see Teresa covering her mouth, her eyes crinkling with amusement. She had the kind of smile that lit up her whole face, and for a moment, Elias forgot all about his almost-fall.

Unable to help himself, he started laughing too, the tension of the trip and the unfamiliarity of this new place dissolving into a lighthearted moment. The cab driver turned in his seat, his brow raised, and in broken English, he asked, "You... ready? Yes?"

They quickly tried to stifle their laughter, though the occasional snicker still escaped as they climbed into the cab and closed the door behind them.

"Definitely ready," Elias said, catching Teresa's eye again, and they both broke into quiet chuckles once more.

As the cab weaved through the winding streets of Bucharest, the laughter between them gradually faded into a comfortable silence, but the lightness lingered. It felt good to laugh, Elias realized, especially with someone like Teresa. She had a way of easing the heaviness he carried, even in small moments like this.

By the time they arrived at the hotel, the laughter had worked its magic, leaving them both in higher spirits. The world suddenly seemed a little less intimidating, and Elias was grateful for the unexpected joy that Teresa had brought to an otherwise tense journey.

As they stepped out of the cab, Elias took in the sight of their hotel with wide-eyed admiration. The building stood tall and imposing, its stone walls bearing the marks of centuries gone by. The architecture was reminiscent of an old-world castle, with turrets and intricate stonework that climbed toward the sky. Ivy trailed along the walls, framing arched windows that seemed to glow warmly in the evening light.

Despite its age, the hotel exuded an undeniable charm, as if each stone had been meticulously placed to evoke a sense of both grandeur and mystery. Large iron lanterns flanked the entrance, their soft glow casting dancing shadows that played across the cobblestone pathway leading up to the carved wooden doors. The lobby was no less impressive—vaulted ceilings adorned with elaborate chandeliers, their crystal droplets catching the light in a dazzling display. The rich wood paneling and plush furnishings created an atmosphere that was both regal and inviting.

Yet, as classic as the hotel appeared, it had all the trappings of modern comfort. Sleek touches were subtly woven into the historic design, blending old-world charm with the conveniences of the present. A modern fireplace flickered in the corner, surrounded by velvet chairs in deep jewel tones, while discreet elevators waited to carry guests up to their rooms. The polished floors were immaculately clean, and the air carried a faint, pleasant scent of lavender and cedar.

Elias couldn't help but be captivated by the setting, its timeless elegance leaving him momentarily speechless. He glanced over at Teresa, who seemed equally entranced, her eyes roaming over the exquisite details of their surroundings.

"This place... it's incredible," Elias murmured, taking in every inch of the lobby. "It feels like stepping into another time, but... somehow it's all so comfortable."

Teresa smiled, nodding in agreement. "It's a perfect blend. Old but modern, grand but warm." She ran her fingers along the edge of a marble pillar, her gaze thoughtful. "It's almost magical."

Elias chuckled softly. "Well, here's to hoping our stay will be more enchanting than eerie."

They shared a smile, the warmth of the hotel already settling into their bones. Whatever lay ahead in their journey, they both felt a sense of calm here, as if the very walls of the hotel were welcoming them into its history and secrets, urging them to rest before the challenges that awaited them.

After checking in, Teresa led the way as they made their way up the grand, winding staircase to the second floor, where their rooms awaited. She had reserved two separate rooms for them, though they were conveniently adjacent, connected by a small shared balcony overlooking the town. It was a thoughtful arrangement, giving each of them privacy while keeping them close enough to easily meet and discuss their plans.

Once they reached their rooms, they parted briefly to unpack and freshen up. Elias took in his surroundings as he unzipped his bag, impressed by the rich, elegant decor. The room held the same old-world charm as the lobby—heavy, dark wood furniture, thick tapestries with intricate designs, and high windows that let in the soft glow of the street lamps below. But the room also had a modern touch with plush bedding, dimmable lights, and a spacious, newly renovated bathroom.

After unpacking, Elias met Teresa in the dining area downstairs, where they shared a cozy, candlelit dinner. Their conversation flowed easily, punctuated by laughter and lighthearted stories. It was as if the tension of their journey had lifted, replaced by the warmth of good food and the comfort of each other's company. They shared tales from their pasts, Teresa recounting some of her more humorous adventures with a twinkle in her eye, and Elias reminiscing about his childhood with a sense of nostalgia.

The evening felt almost normal, a rare and welcome reprieve from the darker mysteries surrounding them.

As they finished their meal, Elias stood up and, almost on instinct, hugged Teresa. It was a gentle embrace, filled with gratitude and camaraderie. "Thank you for being here," he said softly. "I don't think I could do this alone."

Teresa returned the hug, smiling. "You're not alone, Elias. We're in this together. But for now, I think a good night's sleep will do us both some good."

Elias nodded, feeling a renewed sense of calm. "Agreed. I'll see you in the morning."

With that, they parted ways, each retreating to their respective rooms. As Elias closed the door behind him, he felt a sense of peace settle over him, the anticipation of the journey ahead no longer as daunting. He knew he was exactly where he needed to be, and with Teresa by his side, he felt ready for whatever tomorrow would bring.

That night, as Elias drifted off to sleep in his quiet, grand hotel room, the weight of exhaustion pulled him under swiftly. But no sooner had he closed his eyes than the familiar nightmare gripped him, thrusting him back into that dreadful place between dreams and reality.

In the dim haze, his parents appeared before him once more, their faces twisted in agony. They reached out toward him, mouths moving, but no sound escaped. He could see his father's eyes, wide with terror, as if trying to convey something urgent, something Elias needed to understand. His mother's lips were forming words, her expression frantic, but before she could speak, an unseen force seemed to clutch at her, pulling her back.

Elias's heart pounded as he watched, frozen in place, unable to move toward them. His parents were screaming silently, their faces contorted in pain, their hands outstretched, grasping at nothing. The air around them grew thick with darkness, swirling like smoke, until it enveloped them completely. And then, out of the shadows, a figure emerged, cloaked in shadow and whispering in a language Elias could barely hear, let alone understand.

The figure's voice grew louder, chanting something that seemed to echo through the vast darkness. With every word, his parents' agonized expressions began to soften, as though a wave of calm washed over them. Their screaming ceased, replaced by a strange, eerie stillness. The figure's hand lifted toward them, and slowly, his parents' faces relaxed, their bodies no longer writhing in pain.

Elias strained to see the figure more clearly, his heart racing as he finally caught a glimpse of its face. The figure's features shifted, flickering between shadows and light, until it took the unmistakable form of his uncle Drago.

Elias's breath caught, a wave of confusion and fear rising within him. Drago's face was calm, almost serene, as if in control of whatever force had been torturing his parents. But before Elias could reach out, before he could cry out in recognition, the figure began to dissipate, Drago's face melting away into darkness.

In an instant, his parents vanished, the dark void swallowing them whole, leaving Elias alone in the suffocating silence. His heart hammered as he struggled to see, to reach out, but all around him was endless blackness. He was trapped, adrift in an empty abyss, the haunting image of Drago and his parents seared into his mind.

With a sudden jolt, Elias awoke, his body drenched in sweat, his chest heaving. The silence of the room closed in around him, but the terror lingered, the echoes of his parents' agony still fresh in his mind. Drago... his uncle was more entangled in this mystery than he'd ever imagined.

Elias sat up, running a hand through his damp hair. He knew now, without a doubt, that he couldn't delay any longer. Whatever was happening, whatever dark force had his parents in its grip, Drago was at the center of it all. And Elias was determined to uncover the truth, no matter what it took.

Elias sat up in bed, his heart still pounding from the nightmare, when he heard a soft knock on his door. The sound jolted him, pulling him back to reality, though the fear and confusion from the dream still clung to him like a shroud.

He got up, crossed the room, and opened the door to find Teresa standing there, her face creased with concern. "Are you okay, Elias?" she asked gently, her voice soft but filled with worry. "I heard you screaming..."

He swallowed, nodding as he gestured for her to come in. "I'm... I'm fine, just had a nightmare," he managed, though he knew his words didn't carry much conviction. The dream had shaken him deeply, and he couldn't push it from his mind. He led her to the spacious sitting area where a grand, vintage couch took up most of the space, its plush cushions inviting them to sit and talk.

As they settled onto the couch, Elias could still feel his hands trembling, his mind racing with the image of his uncle's face, flickering like a specter in his parents' nightmare. He took a deep breath, trying to calm himself, before he began recounting the dream to Teresa, his voice low and unsteady.

"It was my parents again," he said, his gaze fixed on the pattern of the rug beneath his feet. "They were... they were in pain, worse than before. My father was trying to say something, but I couldn't hear him. And my mother—she was reaching out, mouthing words, but then something... something pulled her back, like she was trapped."

Teresa listened intently, her expression growing darker as he continued.

"They were screaming," he said, his voice barely a whisper, "but then this... figure appeared. It was chanting something, and as it did, they seemed calmer. The pain, the agony... it stopped. And then, the figure—" he hesitated, glancing at Teresa, as though saying it aloud would make it more real. "It was my uncle Drago."

Teresa's eyes widened slightly, though she didn't interrupt. She seemed to be absorbing every word, her own mind working through the implications of his dream.

Elias shook his head, frustration and fear clouding his thoughts. "But was he helping them or... controlling them somehow? I can't tell. And when I saw him, he just... disappeared. Everything went dark."

He leaned back on the couch, rubbing his temples as the weight of it all settled over him again. "I don't know if Drago is a friend or a foe, Teresa. I don't know what he's capable of, or what he has to gain from all of this. But he's involved. I'm certain of that now."

Teresa reached out, placing a reassuring hand on his shoulder. "Dreams can sometimes show us things we can't see when we're awake. They're warnings, messages... even memories we don't fully understand yet. Whatever this means, we'll figure it out."

Her voice was steady, grounding him, and Elias felt a flicker of relief. With Teresa by his side, he didn't feel quite so lost in the darkness.

"I'm glad you're here," he admitted, his gaze meeting hers. "I don't think I could face this alone."

She gave him a small, reassuring smile. "You're not alone, Elias. Whatever Drago's intentions are, we'll uncover the truth. And we'll do it together."

They sat in silence for a moment, the gravity of the journey ahead settling between them. The question remained, gnawing at Elias's mind: Was Drago a savior—or a threat?

Elias's hands trembled, the residual fear from the nightmare lingering within him. Teresa noticed, her gaze softening, and without a word, she reached over, taking his hands into hers. She laced their fingers together, offering silent comfort and grounding him in the warmth of her touch. Her presence made him feel safer, and for the first time in a long time, he felt the heavy weight of his worries begin to lift.

As he looked into her eyes, a sense of longing stirred within him, a feeling that went beyond companionship and friendship. It was something deeper, something he had tried to ignore but couldn't any longer. He leaned toward her, and as if drawn by an unspoken understanding, she closed the distance, her lips meeting his. The kiss was gentle at first, a moment of solace, but quickly grew in intensity as they surrendered to the undeniable connection between them. She held the back of his head, fingers entwined in his hair, and he felt himself let go of all the fears that had plagued him.

That night, they found comfort in each other, a release from the weight of uncertainty and the darkness surrounding them. They came together, their fears and hopes merging as one, their connection providing solace and strength.

As the first light of morning streamed through the window, illuminating the room in a warm glow, Elias stirred awake. He looked over at Teresa, her face softened by sleep, and felt a sense of peace he hadn't felt in years. She opened her eyes, meeting his gaze with a smile, and without needing to say a word, they shared another tender moment, rekindling the passion and closeness they had discovered the night before.

In those quiet moments of morning light, with all the world's mysteries temporarily set aside, Elias felt whole—grounded and ready to face whatever lay ahead, with Teresa by his side.

As Elias lay beside Teresa, watching the sunlight dance across her face, he felt a warmth that reached beyond simple attraction or companionship. It was something deeper, a feeling he hadn't allowed himself to experience in a long time. The realization settled over him like a quiet revelation—he was falling in love with Teresa.

This truth brought a surge of emotion, and as he stirred, it seemed to wake her. She opened her eyes, blinking against the soft light, and when her gaze met his, she gave him the warmest, most radiant smile he'd ever seen. His heart melted, the last defenses he'd been holding onto slipping away.

"Good morning," he said softly, unable to contain the warmth in his voice.

"Good morning," she replied, her eyes sparkling as she leaned in and kissed him, a gentle, lingering kiss that held both tenderness and promise.

In that moment, the fears and uncertainties of their journey faded, if only for a while. Here, in the warmth of their shared affection, Elias felt a new strength, an unspoken vow to protect her and to face whatever darkness lay ahead together. They lay there, wrapped in each other's presence, savoring the quiet peace of the morning

When they finally rose from the comfort of their room, Elias and Teresa exchanged a look of understanding. They knew today was the day they would face the unknowns waiting at his uncle Drago's home, but before that, they agreed they'd enjoy a peaceful breakfast together —a moment of calm before venturing into the storm of unanswered questions.

They dressed quickly, their expressions softened by the shared warmth of the morning, and headed downstairs to the hotel's dining area. The morning light streamed through tall, arched windows, illuminating the space in a warm, inviting glow. The dining room was adorned with polished wood tables and soft linens, the aroma of fresh coffee and pastries filling the air.

As they sat down and glanced over the menu, Elias found himself more at ease than he had been in days. They ordered an assortment of breakfast dishes, and soon, their table was filled with warm pastries, fresh fruit, and perfectly brewed coffee. The flavors were rich and satisfying, reminiscent of the wonderful dinner they'd shared the night before.

They chatted quietly as they ate, their conversation light and filled with moments of shared laughter. It felt like a reprieve, a slice of normalcy in the midst of their quest. Teresa's laughter was infectious, her presence a steady comfort to Elias, and he couldn't help but feel grateful to have her by his side.

As they finished their meal, a renewed sense of purpose filled them both. The time had come to seek the answers they'd traveled so far to find. With one last shared look, they rose from the table, ready to confront whatever secrets Uncle Drago's home would reveal.

As Elias checked his phone, he noticed a new message waiting in his voicemail. It was from Drago. He listened, his expression growing thoughtful as he heard his uncle's gruff voice inviting him to come over the following afternoon. But one detail sent a chill down his spine —the timestamp on the message matched the exact time he had woken up from his nightmare. He shared this strange coincidence with Teresa, who raised her eyebrows in surprise, clearly as taken aback as he was.

"What are the odds?" she murmured, a hint of intrigue in her voice.

They exchanged a look of understanding before deciding to make the most of their day. They had some time before meeting Drago, and exploring Bucharest together seemed like the perfect distraction from the mysterious weight of his dream and the peculiar timing of the message.

They spent the morning strolling through the winding streets, hand in hand, laughing and talking as if they didn't have a care in the world. For a while, they forgot about curses, dark dreams, and family mysteries, allowing themselves to be absorbed by the charm of the city around them. They visited bustling markets, admired historic architecture, and wandered through quaint alleys filled with colorful shops. At one point, they stopped at a small, cozy café where they shared a rich, aromatic coffee, their laughter mixing with the hum of the city.

As they continued their walk, they passed a shop window filled with beautiful antiques. An elegant heart-shaped necklace, delicately crafted and glinting softly in the light, caught Elias's eye. Without hesitation, he went inside and purchased it, feeling a sense of warmth at the thought of giving it to Teresa.

"Here," he said, turning to her with a smile as he held the necklace in his hands. "I thought it would look perfect on you."

Teresa's eyes sparkled as he clasped it around her neck, her fingers brushing his as she admired the necklace. It looked as though it was meant for her, resting gracefully against her collarbone, the antique heart pendant catching the light.

"It's beautiful," she said softly, touching the pendant with a smile. "Thank you, Elias."

He couldn't help but think how perfect she looked, her happiness contagious as she beamed at him. In that moment, Elias felt as though nothing could ruin this day. Whatever mysteries awaited them tomorrow, he knew he'd remember today as a bright, precious memory, a moment suspended in time amidst all the darkness.

Elias took a deep breath, feeling his heart pound as he looked into Teresa's eyes, the words forming on his lips almost of their own accord. "You know," he began, his voice low and a little raspy, "I know this is sudden, but... I love you, Teresa. And yes, I know it's quick, but I can't help it."

He reached out, gently cupping her hands in his. His gaze was earnest, vulnerable, as he bared his heart to her. For a moment, he feared he might have overstepped, but then she looked up at him, her own eyes shimmering with emotion.

"Oh, Elias," she whispered, her voice trembling slightly. "I love you too. From the moment we met, I think I knew. I tried to ignore it, tried to focus on what we were here to do, but I can't deny it anymore."

A wave of relief and joy washed over Elias as her words sank in. He pulled her closer, and they embraced, the world around them fading as they stood together in that quiet moment. It felt as if everything had led them to this, a place of warmth and certainty, a refuge amidst the chaos they were facing.

Their hands stayed intertwined as they continued to walk through the city, but now, each step held a new kind of purpose, a shared promise that strengthened them both. Whatever awaited them with Drago, with the mysteries of the cane and Elias's family, they would face it together, bound by a love that had sparked unexpectedly but felt as if it had been destined all along.

As they approached the hotel, Elias noticed a sleek, black limousine parked out front, its polished surface gleaming under the midday sun. He raised an eyebrow, nudging Teresa with a grin. "Looks like we have some celebrities staying here today."

Teresa chuckled, her eyes twinkling mischievously. "Or maybe it's Dracula himself, coming to visit," she teased, a playful smirk on her lips.

They laughed together as they walked into the lobby, the warm glow of the hotel welcoming them back. But then, just as they crossed the threshold, Elias felt a jolt, as though a bolt of lightning had struck him. His heart froze, his laughter fading, and the world seemed to narrow down to the sight before him.

Standing across the lobby, partially shadowed by the dim lighting, was the figure from his dream—the very same figure he'd seen looming over his parents, chanting in his nightmares.

"Uncle Drago?" he whispered, his voice barely audible, his heart pounding with a mixture of fear and disbelief.

The figure turned, and Elias's heart skipped a beat as he came face-to-face with the man he hadn't seen in years. Drago's face was worn but intense, his eyes dark and piercing. He held himself with an air of quiet authority, an unsettling presence that seemed to fill the room. And then, in a voice deep and resonant, he spoke.

"Hello, Elias."

The words hung in the air, charged with a strange, electric energy. Elias's mind raced with questions, emotions swirling as he tried to reconcile the man before him with the haunting figure from his dream. Teresa's grip tightened on his hand, steadying him as he took a tentative step forward.

"Uncle Drago… what are you doing here?" Elias managed, his voice wavering.

Drago's lips curved into a slight smile, his gaze shifting briefly to Teresa before returning to Elias. "I thought it was time we spoke... face to face." His eyes seemed to flicker with an unreadable emotion, and in that moment, Elias couldn't tell if he was looking at a friend or a foe.

The air grew thick with tension, and Elias's mind echoed with the haunting question he had wrestled with all morning: Was Drago here to help—or to pull him further into the darkness?

Elias's thoughts spiraled, his mind racing with unanswered questions, but Teresa's voice cut through the fog, grounding him.

"Hello," she said, stepping forward and extending her hand to Drago, her expression calm but assertive. "It's a pleasure to finally meet you, sir."

Drago turned to her, his imposing figure somehow softened by her composed greeting. He was a striking man, his broad shoulders and tall, commanding stance giving him an air of quiet strength. His deep brown eyes studied her with a mix of curiosity and respect, and a lock of dark hair fell across his face, adding an air of mystery to his features.

He reached out, taking Teresa's hand with a surprising gentleness, as though aware of his own strength. His handshake was brief but firm, respectful yet restrained, as if he held back a deeper intensity beneath his calm exterior.

"Teresa," he said, his voice low and resonant. "I've heard much about you. I'm pleased you're here. Elias is... fortunate to have someone so steadfast by his side."

Drago's words held a weight, a significance that Elias couldn't quite decipher, but he felt a surge of gratitude for Teresa. She had managed to bridge the tension between them, bringing a sense of calm to the charged encounter. Her unwavering presence reminded him that he wasn't alone, even in the face of his family's deepest secrets.

Elias cleared his throat, finally finding his voice. "Uncle Drago... thank you for agreeing to see us."

Drago's eyes flickered with something unreadable, his gaze shifting between the two of them. "It was time," he replied simply, his voice holding a note of finality. "There are things you need to understand, Elias. Things that have waited too long in the shadows."

The weight of his words settled over them, and Elias felt a sense of foreboding, but he steeled himself. With Teresa beside him, he knew he was ready to confront whatever secrets Drago held.

Drago gestured for them to follow him to a quiet corner of the lobby, where a secluded sitting area offered privacy. He lowered himself into an armchair, his imposing presence softened slightly by the dim, warm lighting. Elias and Teresa took seats across from him, anticipation and apprehension reflected in their expressions.

Elias took a deep breath, breaking the silence. "Uncle Drago... my parents. I've been having dreams about them. They're in pain, calling out to me, but... there's more." He hesitated, glancing at Teresa for reassurance before continuing. "In the last dream, you were there. You were... chanting something. They seemed calmer after, but... it was you. I don't understand."

Drago's eyes darkened, his expression tinged with solemnity, as if he had anticipated this. He sighed, his voice lowering to a near whisper. "The dreams you've been having, Elias... they're more than dreams. They're glimpses, windows into something beyond the ordinary. What you're seeing is real. Your parents... they're trapped."

A chill crawled down Elias's spine, confirming his deepest fears. "Trapped? By what? By whom?"

Drago leaned forward, his eyes grave, his expression darkened with memories long buried. "There are forces at work that your mother's family has been bound to for generations," he began. "Your great-grandparents—long before you or Teresa was born—entered into a pact, a powerful and binding one, with ancient forces to protect the family. It was meant to be a safeguard, but... something went wrong. And now, your parents and I are paying the price."

He took a deep breath, his gaze distant as if seeing those fateful moments play out once more. "I never wanted to be part of it. In fact, I tried to stop it. Your great-grandfather, my own brother... he was obsessed with gaining power, with securing protection for the family at any cost. He believed that by making this pact, he could save the family from dangers he feared but didn't fully understand. But I knew the risks. I could see the darkness in what he was trying to do."

Elias felt a shiver as he listened, the weight of Drago's words heavy in the air.

"I confronted him," Drago continued, his voice lowering as if even now, he feared stirring old forces. "I begged him not to go through with it, to consider the consequences of what he was about to do. But he wouldn't listen. He was blinded by his desire for protection and power. And that night, I was there when he completed the ritual... I tried to stop him. But I was too late."

Drago's hands clenched into fists, his knuckles white. "In the final moments of the pact, when he called upon the ancient forces, I was caught in the circle of power, drawn into the very pact I had tried to prevent. My own brother's actions sealed my fate. I became bound to the curse, rendered immortal, condemned to watch generations of our family pay the price for his choices. For nearly three centuries, I have lived, cursed with the burden of his mistake."

Elias's heart raced, the full weight of Drago's words sinking in. His uncle, whom he had always seen as a mysterious figure on the fringes of the family, was an unwilling participant —a man who had spent nearly 300 years atoning for a choice he had never made.

"A pact?" Elias repeated, struggling to wrap his mind around it. "Why didn't anyone tell me? Why was I kept in the dark?"

Drago's face softened, regret shadowing his expression. "To shield you, Elias. Your mother only learned the truth after your grandfather passed. She wanted to protect you from the same burdens she carried, believing she could manage it alone." He looked away, his voice heavy. "But in truth, none of us can face this alone."

Teresa, who had been listening intently, leaned forward. "Is there a way to save them?" she asked, her voice steady and resolute. "To bring them back?"

Drago's gaze turned to her, a flicker of respect in his eyes. "There may be a way," he replied. "But it will require strength, courage... and a willingness to face the darkness head-on. Elias, you'll need the cane. It holds the key to unraveling this curse."

Elias's heart pounded at the mention of the cane. "But what does the cane have to do with any of this? It's just... it was just my mother's."

Drago shook his head. "The cane is more than a keepsake. It's a vessel, a conduit for the power that binds your mother's family to the pact. It was passed down through generations, entrusted to her as a way to control the forces your great-grandparents engaged with. But now, it must pass to you."

Elias felt a shiver of trepidation, the weight of his uncle's words pressing on him. "So... if I take the cane, if I go through with this, I can free my parents?"

Drago's gaze was unwavering, his eyes intense. "Perhaps. But be warned, Elias—this journey will test you, reveal truths about your family that have been buried for generations. There are others who would do anything to keep these secrets hidden."

Teresa placed a steadying hand on Elias's shoulder, her warmth grounding him. "Whatever it takes," she said softly, her voice filled with quiet resolve. "We'll face it together."

Drago nodded, his expression grave. "Very well. If you're ready, then I will guide you. But remember this, Elias—once you step onto this path, there is no turning back."

Elias glanced at Teresa, drawing strength from her steady presence, then turned back to Drago, his determination solidified.

"I'm ready," he said, his voice firm. "Let's do this."

Drago's lips lifted in a faint, sorrowful smile, though his eyes remained shadowed with centuries of grief and regret. "Then we begin."

"But what does this have to do with my family, Drago?" Teresa's voice was calm, though her eyes betrayed the storm of emotions churning within her. "It seems like the same curse that has inflicted so much pain on Elias's family has also affected mine… and my friend Jo."

Drago's face softened as he took in the gravity of Teresa's question. After a brief silence, he spoke again, this time with a tone of sorrow and respect for the past.

"There's a piece of history, Teresa, that has tied our families together more deeply than you know. Your grandfather, long before he settled in the Philippines, was a servant to Elias's family. He was trusted and loyal, and when Elias's great-grandparents traveled to the Philippines on their honeymoon, they brought him along to help with the journey. It was shortly after that trip that the seeds of this pact were sown."

Teresa's brow furrowed, curiosity and surprise flickering in her gaze. She hadn't known of this connection, this bond between her family and Elias's going back generations.

"When they returned to England," Drago continued, "your great-grandfather accompanied them, having become a trusted member of their household. In England, Elias's great-grandparents became drawn to the allure of forbidden practices, ancient secrets they thought they could wield to protect their legacy. Your family, through that bond of loyalty, was drawn into the pact as well, unwittingly bound to the very forces Elias's family had summoned."

Elias listened, a sense of weight settling over him as he began to see how deep the curse's roots stretched.

"But that's not all," Drago added, his voice growing darker. "After they returned to England, your great-grandfather and the rest of the household became involved in strange gatherings, rituals they didn't fully understand. It was in this shadowed world that they crossed paths with Jo's family."

"Jo's family?" Teresa's voice was barely above a whisper, her shock evident.

"Yes," Drago nodded. "Jo's great-grandfather was a bodyguard hired to protect Elias's great-grandmother, who had become increasingly paranoid as she sensed the dark powers gathering around them. Jo's ancestor, though not fully aware of the pact's details, knew something was amiss. Over time, his family was also drawn into the curse, bound by proximity and loyalty, their lives forever intertwined with your own."

Elias clenched his fists, the realization that his family's decisions had trapped others, strangers who had become family by fate, in a centuries-old nightmare.

"So... my family's curse... it was never just ours," Elias murmured, almost to himself.

"No," Drago confirmed, his voice filled with regret. "By the time the pact was completed, the curse had already spread. Your family, Teresa's, and Jo's were all tied together, each line bearing a part of the burden."

Teresa looked at Elias, her hand gripping his tightly. "So it was fate that brought us together... but now, we have the choice to break it."

Elias met her gaze, feeling the depth of that truth resonate within him. Their families had been tied together by forces they hadn't chosen, but here and now, they would fight together to end it.

Drago watched them, a flicker of hope kindling in his ancient, weary eyes. "Yes. And together, you may be the ones who can finally lay this curse to rest, freeing not only your families but everyone who has been caught in its reach."

A sense of purpose filled them, binding them with the strength of generations. Their journey would be perilous, but together, they would face the dark legacy—and bring an end to the curse that had haunted their families for far too long.

Teresa watched Drago carefully, noticing the slight hesitation in his gaze, as if a shadow of uncertainty lingered behind his words. She felt there was something more he wasn't saying, a deeper layer to the story that he hadn't revealed. Gently, she asked, "Drago... is there something else?"

Drago shifted, his expression tightening as if he were grappling with an old, unresolved mystery. "Yes," he admitted slowly, his voice low and filled with the weight of years. "There was a third family... another presence there when the pact was formed. They were part of the household, involved enough to be swept into the curse alongside the others. But after the curse had been released... they vanished without a trace. I have tried, for centuries, to find them, but it's as if they disappeared from the face of the earth."

Elias leaned forward, his curiosity piqued. "A third family? Who were they?"

Drago sighed, as if saying the name itself were a burden he had carried for too long. "Their surname was Ravenwood. They were an old family, one with their own history of strange practices and an affinity for the occult. They had come from Eastern Europe originally, though they had settled in England by the time of the pact. They were trusted advisors, scholars, and keepers of certain... secrets."

Teresa's eyes widened. "The Ravenwoods... they were involved, too?"

"Yes," Drago replied, nodding. "They were integral to the ritual. Your great-grandparents believed that with the Ravenwoods' knowledge, they could invoke ancient protection without consequence. But after the pact was completed and the curse released, the Ravenwoods vanished, leaving behind only whispers and rumors. They may have sensed the curse's full weight before anyone else, perhaps even found a way to shield themselves. But as for where they went, or how they avoided the curse's grasp... it's a mystery I've never been able to solve. Their secrets are buried too deeply."

Teresa glanced at Elias, the gravity of this revelation sinking in. "So they may have had a way to break free from it?"

"Possibly," Drago admitted. "They knew things—ancient rites and rituals, protective spells. If there is a key to breaking the curse, it may lie within their knowledge. If we could find any trace of them, any descendants... it could be the answer we've been searching for."

Elias felt a surge of determination. "Then maybe that's where we start. If they escaped, they might hold the last piece we need."

Drago looked at them both, a glimmer of hope mingling with uncertainty. "I've spent lifetimes searching for them to no avail. But perhaps... perhaps with your fresh eyes, your conviction, you might succeed where I could not."

Teresa's hand tightened around Elias's. "Then let's find them. We're closer than anyone has ever been. We have to try."

Drago nodded, his face filled with a mix of relief and lingering tension. "Then our journey gains a new purpose. The Ravenwoods may hold the key to unraveling everything."

Elias took a steadying breath, his gaze firm as he looked at Drago and Teresa. "Before anything else, we have to help my parents. Finding the Ravenwoods might give us answers, but my parents are suffering right now. We can't lose focus on that."

Drago nodded, his expression solemn. "You're right, Elias. The curse is already claiming them, and the longer we wait, the tighter its grip will become. Every moment counts."

Teresa reached out, placing a reassuring hand on Elias's shoulder. "I'm with you. Your parents come first. We'll do whatever it takes to free them."

Drago looked between them, his eyes heavy with understanding and determination. "If we can free your parents, Elias, we may weaken the curse enough to make finding the Ravenwoods possible. But we must act quickly and with caution. The forces we're dealing with are as old as they are unpredictable."

Elias gave a resolute nod, feeling the support of both Drago and Teresa beside him. "Then we'll move forward—together."

In that moment, a shared determination bound them. They would face the darkness surrounding his family, uncover the secrets buried in the curse, and, above all, fight to save his parents.

As their journey to confront the curse deepened, Elias, Teresa, and Drago found themselves combing through the dense, shadowed paths of the Black Forest in Germany. Drago had led them there, believing that the forest held ancient powers, remnants of rituals and old magic that had once protected families from malevolent forces.

Their exploration took days, winding through overgrown trails and crumbling ruins hidden beneath the towering trees. The forest seemed alive with whispers and a strange, pulsing energy, as though it held secrets waiting to be discovered. Drago had a map, one passed down for generations, marked with symbols and places of power. According to him, there was a fabled relic hidden somewhere in the depths of the forest—an enchanted stone imbued with protection spells, something their ancestors had sought before finalizing the pact.

The trio pressed on, determined to find the relic. Teresa's presence was a comfort to Elias, her steady calm balancing the strange tension in the forest. They trudged through brambles and uneven terrain, the shadows lengthening as they ventured deeper, until finally, they reached an ancient stone circle hidden in a grove. The circle was surrounded by weathered stone pillars, each etched with runes so faint they were barely visible.

In the center of the circle lay the relic: a small, dark stone set within a metal clasp, faintly glowing in the dim light. It was unmistakably magical, emanating a warmth that seemed to chase away the surrounding shadows.

Drago's voice was reverent as he approached it. "This... this is the talisman. It's older than the curse itself, created to ward off dark forces. Your ancestors sought it out but never found it in time. But now... it's here, waiting for us."

Elias stepped forward, and as his fingers brushed the talisman, he felt a surge of energy—calming yet powerful, like a protective force surrounding him. Teresa joined him, placing her hand over his as they held the relic together. Drago whispered an incantation, activating its dormant power.

With the talisman in hand, Elias felt a renewed confidence. The relic's protective magic would help them counteract the curse's darkest forces. He could sense the relic connecting with the cane he carried, as if the two pieces of magic were fusing, working together to strengthen their bond against the shadows awaiting them.

Armed with this newfound power, the three of them prepared to leave the Black Forest. The relic's protection filled them with hope and a shared determination to finally break the curse that had plagued their families for so long.

As they prepared to leave Germany for England, Elias, Teresa, and Drago booked a late evening flight, hoping the cover of night would offer them some peace after the intense ritual in the Black Forest. They were exhausted but resolute, each of them aware that the final step awaited them on English soil. Teresa, however, had started feeling a bit off, a faint nausea settling over her, though she brushed it off as nerves. She focused on the task ahead, not wanting to worry Elias, but she couldn't ignore the slight waves of dizziness that washed over her from time to time.

The flight from Germany to England was tense and quiet, with Elias and Drago deep in thought, preparing for the challenges ahead. Teresa tried to rest, leaning her head back against the seat, but an unsettling nausea began to churn within her. She attributed it to the stress of the curse-breaking journey, the lingering energy from the ritual, or even the strange magic they had encountered in the forest.

At one point, Elias noticed her pale complexion and took her hand gently. "Are you okay?" he asked, his voice soft with concern.

Teresa forced a smile, nodding. "I think it's just the flight. I'll be fine," she assured him, squeezing his hand. She didn't want him to worry, not now, when so much depended on their strength and focus.

By the time they landed in England, Teresa felt the wave of nausea subside somewhat, though a strange heaviness lingered in her body. The trio made their way to the hotel they had booked in a small, secluded village near the ancient chapel, the location of their final ritual.

The hotel was a quaint, ivy-covered building nestled among trees on the edge of the village, its exterior shrouded in mist that gave it an almost dreamlike quality. Inside, the lobby was warm and welcoming, with old wood paneling, a crackling fireplace, and the scent of fresh herbs lingering in the air. The receptionist, an elderly woman with a warm smile, handed them their keys, and they each went to their respective rooms to prepare for the next day.

As Teresa reached her room, the nausea returned, stronger this time, making her grip the edge of the doorframe to steady herself. She closed her eyes, taking a few slow breaths, willing the feeling to pass. Her mind was filled with images of the ritual, the dark energy they'd encountered, and the strength it would take to face it all again.

Elias noticed her hesitation and walked over, concern etched on his face. "Teresa, you look really pale," he said gently. "Maybe you should rest a bit."

She nodded, grateful for his support. "I think you're right. It's probably just the aftereffects of everything we went through in the Black Forest." She managed a faint smile. "I'll be fine after some sleep."

Elias hesitated but finally hugged her, his arms warm and comforting. "Get some rest. We'll face whatever comes next together," he promised, his voice filled with quiet strength.

That night, Teresa's sleep was restless. She awoke several times, feeling flushed and queasy, and in the early hours of the morning, she found herself pacing her room, trying to shake off the strange sensations. She'd had unusual dreams, filled with symbols from the forest, images of the ancient relic they'd discovered, and flashes of warmth that felt oddly comforting. She placed a hand on her stomach, an inexplicable sense of peace settling over her.

The next morning, she met Elias and Drago in the hotel's small breakfast area. She felt a little better after some tea, but her appetite was nearly nonexistent. Elias looked at her with concern, noting the slight paleness in her cheeks.

"Are you sure you're okay?" he asked again, his hand resting on hers.

Teresa took a sip of her tea, trying to push away the lingering nausea. "I'll be fine," she replied, her voice steady but soft. "It's just... this journey has taken a toll, I suppose."

Drago, perceptive as ever, gave her an understanding nod. "Magic like this doesn't pass without leaving its mark. But I believe you'll regain your strength soon," he said, his voice calm and reassuring.

They finished breakfast, and with Teresa determined to push past her discomfort, they gathered their supplies and made their way to the ancient chapel. The sense of anticipation hung heavily over them, but with each step, Teresa found herself drawing strength from the warmth within her, a quiet resolve growing alongside the slight sickness she couldn't shake.

The journey to free Elias's parents had brought Elias, Teresa, and Drago to an abandoned chapel deep within an ancient estate in England. The chapel, hidden within a misty forest, was overgrown and decayed, with ivy crawling up its stone walls and shattered stained-glass windows casting faint, colored shadows across the floor. This was the place where

Elias's great-grandparents had first sealed the pact, the birthplace of the curse. Now, it would be the site of its undoing.

Inside, the air was thick and heavy, filled with an oppressive energy that clung to their skin. At the center of the room stood a large stone altar, darkened with age and etched with symbols that seemed to pulse with a faint, sinister glow as they approached. Shadows flickered along the walls, almost as if they were alive, and whispers seemed to rise from the very stones, a chorus of voices angry and unwelcoming.

Elias took a deep breath, steadying himself. He held the enchanted cane in one hand and the protective relic they had found in the Black Forest in the other. The relic emitted a faint warmth, its power growing in response to the darkness that surrounded them. Teresa and Drago took their positions beside him, forming a triangle around the altar, each of them bracing for the confrontation to come.

Drago began to chant in a low, rhythmic voice, speaking in the ancient language of their ancestors. The words vibrated through the air, stirring the shadows around them. As he chanted, the relic in Elias's hand began to glow brighter, casting a protective light over the trio and pushing back the darkness. Teresa stood steady, her gaze unwavering, her hand reaching out to touch Elias's shoulder, grounding him.

The shadows recoiled from the relic's light, hissing as if in pain, but they did not retreat. Instead, they began to gather, swirling around the altar like a vortex, coalescing into dark, writhing shapes. And then, out of the darkness, the spectral forms of Elias's parents appeared, bound by thick chains made of pure shadow. Their faces were twisted in agony, their eyes filled with a haunting plea as they reached out toward Elias.

Elias felt his heart break at the sight. "Mom… Dad…" he whispered, his voice choked with emotion. He tightened his grip on the cane, feeling the relic's warmth pulse through him, strengthening his resolve. He knew what he had to do.

"By the power of this cane and the bloodline it binds," Elias called out, his voice firm and commanding, "I command you to release them! Your hold over my family ends here and now!"

The shadows hissed in defiance, their voices echoing through the chapel in a cacophony of rage. The chains around his parents tightened, as if trying to strangle the last remnants of life from them. But the relic in Elias's hand blazed with light, pushing the shadows back and forcing the chains to weaken, cracks appearing along their length.

Teresa began chanting, lending her strength to the ritual. Her voice was strong and clear, weaving protection around them, fortifying their defenses against the curse's wrath. She held tightly to Elias's shoulder, her presence a steady anchor in the turbulent energy swirling around them.

Drago's chanting intensified, his voice rising to a fevered pitch. "Let this curse be broken! By the power of blood and the will of those who have come to end it!"

The shadows screamed, their forms contorting, but they continued to resist, clawing at the protective light of the relic. Elias could feel the power in the cane surge, responding to his determination. He lifted it higher, focusing every ounce of his will on freeing his parents from the curse's grasp.

The light from the cane and relic merged, creating a blinding beam that shot toward the altar, striking the chains and shattering them in an explosion of shadow and light. The curse's hold began to unravel, the darkness receding as the power of the relic forced it back. Bit by bit, Elias's parents' forms became clearer, the pain in their faces easing as the last remnants of the curse dissolved.

With one final, agonized shriek, the shadows disintegrated, dissipating into wisps of smoke that faded into the air. The oppressive energy lifted, leaving the chapel in a hushed, almost sacred silence.

Elias dropped the cane, rushing to his parents' side as they collapsed on the altar, finally freed from their visible chains of darkness. Tears streamed down his face as he took his mother's hand, her touch warm and alive.

"Elias..." she whispered, her voice weak but filled with love. "You saved us."

His father looked at him with pride, his expression filled with relief and gratitude. "Thank you, son. You... you've done what we could not."

But just as the relief washed over them, his father's face darkened, a shadow of concern flickering in his eyes. He glanced over Elias's shoulder, his gaze wary. "But this... this is not the end," he said, his voice thick with urgency.

Elias turned quickly, a chill creeping up his spine. Though the chains had vanished, the air remained heavy with an eerie, pulsing energy. The shadows, which they thought had been destroyed, began to reform at the edges of the room, dark tendrils snaking along the walls, filling the chapel with an ominous presence.

Drago stepped forward, his face pale as he took in the sight. "The curse... it's still rooted here," he murmured, his voice filled with dread. "It hasn't been fully broken. The darkness was only severed from your parents temporarily—it still clings to this place, feeding off an ancient bond."

"What does that mean?" Elias asked, fear seeping into his voice. He tightened his grip on the cane, but it felt oddly cold, its power somehow diminished.

Drago's eyes were grave as he turned to Elias and Teresa. "It means that breaking the visible chains wasn't enough. This curse runs far deeper—it's bound not just by ritual, but by bloodlines, intertwined through more than one family. There's a part of the curse we can't touch, a force that ties it to someone else..."

Elias's mind raced, pieces of Drago's story beginning to make sense. "The Ravenwoods," he whispered, the name ringing with an almost supernatural weight.

Drago nodded slowly. "Yes... the Ravenwoods. They were part of the original ritual. They vanished after the curse was released, possibly protecting themselves. But their family bloodline is connected to the pact just as ours is." His eyes glinted with the realization. "If we're to destroy this curse completely, we need the Ravenwoods. Without their bloodline, the ritual remains incomplete."

Teresa's face hardened with determination as she looked at Elias. "Then we have to find them," she said, her voice steady. "If they hold the missing piece, we can't finish this without them."

Elias's parents looked at him, their faces etched with concern and hope. His mother's voice trembled as she spoke. "Elias... if they're the key, you have to find them. The curse's hold will weaken us again if it remains unchecked."

Drago placed a hand on Elias's shoulder. "Finding the Ravenwoods is the only way to free your family fully, to prevent the curse from regaining strength. I've searched for them for centuries, but maybe, with all we've uncovered, you'll succeed where I failed."

Elias looked at Teresa, seeing the same fierce resolve in her eyes that he felt. "Then we'll search for them together," he said, his voice steady. "We'll find the Ravenwoods... and we'll end this curse once and for all."

With a final look at the lingering shadows in the chapel, Elias felt the weight of the unfinished task settle over him. The journey wasn't over, but he knew that they now held a glimmer of hope—one last chance to break the curse forever.

www.ingramcontent.com/pod-product-compliance
Ingram Content Group UK Ltd.
Pitfield, Milton Keynes, MK11 3LW, UK
UKHW050150201224
452606UK00008B/182

9 798330 623969